EASY INSTRUMENTAL DUETS    ALTO SAXES

# HIT SONGS FOR TWO

Arrangements by Peter Deneff

ISBN 978-1-5400-1278-4

HAL•LEONARD®
7777 W. BLUEMOUND RD. P.O. BOX 13819 MILWAUKEE, WI 53213

Visit Hal Leonard Online at
**www.halleonard.com**

# CONTENTS

# ALL ABOUT THAT BASS

ALTO SAXES

Words and Music by KEVIN KADISH
and MEGHAN TRAINOR

# ALL OF ME

ALTO SAXES

Words and Music by JOHN STEPHENS
and TOBY GAD

# BRAVE

ALTO SAXES

Words and Music by SARA BAREILLES
and JACK ANTONOFF

# BUDAPEST

ALTO SAXES

Words and Music by GEORGE BARNETT
and JOEL POTT

# CAN'T STOP THE FEELING

from TROLLS

ALTO SAXES

Words and Music by JUSTIN TIMBERLAKE,
MAX MARTIN and SHELLBACK

# GRENADE

ALTO SAXES

Words and Music by BRUNO MARS,
ARI LEVINE, PHILIP LAWRENCE,
BRODY BROWN, CLAUDE KELLY
and ANDREW WYATT

**Moderately**

# HEY, SOUL SISTER

ALTO SAXES

Words and Music by PAT MONAHAN,
ESPEN LIND and AMUND BJORKLUND

# HOME

ALTO SAXES

Words and Music by GREG HOLDEN
and DREW PEARSON

# I WILL WAIT

ALTO SAXES

Words and Music by
MUMFORD & SONS

**Moderately**

# LET HER GO

ALTO SAXES

Words and Music by
MICHAEL DAVID ROSENBERG

**CODA**

D.S. al Coda

# LET IT GO

ALTO SAXES

Words and Music by JAMES BAY
and PAUL BARRY

# 100 YEARS

**ALTO SAXES**

Words and Music by
JOHN ONDRASIK

*rit.*

*rit.*

# POKER FACE

ALTO SAXES

Words and Music by STEFANI GERMANOTTA
and RedOne

# ROYALS

ALTO SAXES

Words and Music by ELLA YELICH-O'CONNOR
and JOEL LITTLE

(small note optional)

# SAY SOMETHING

ALTO SAXES

Words and Music by IAN AXEL,
CHAD VACCARINO and MIKE CAMPBELL

# SHAKE IT OFF

ALTO SAXES

Words and Music by TAYLOR SWIFT,
MAX MARTIN and SHELLBACK

# SHAPE OF YOU

ALTO SAXES

Words and Music by ED SHEERAN,
KEVIN BRIGGS, KANDI BURRUSS,
TAMEKA COTTLE, STEVE MAC
and JOHNNY McDAID

**Moderately fast**

# SKYFALL

from the Motion Picture SKYFALL

ALTO SAXES

Words and Music by ADELE ADKINS
and PAUL EPWORTH

# SOME NIGHTS

ALTO SAXES

Words and Music by JEFF BHASKER,
ANDREW DOST, JACK ANTONOFF
and NATE RUESS

# STAY WITH ME

ALTO SAXES

Words and Music by SAM SMITH,
JAMES NAPIER, WILLIAM EDWARD PHILLIPS,
TOM PETTY and JEFF LYNNE

# STORY OF MY LIFE

ALTO SAXES

Words and Music by JAMIE SCOTT,
JOHN HENRY RYAN, JULIAN BUNETTA,
HARRY STYLES, LIAM PAYNE, LOUIS TOMLINSON,
NIALL HORAN and ZAIN MALIK

# VIVA LA VIDA

ALTO SAXES

Words and Music by GUY BERRYMAN,
JON BUCKLAND, WILL CHAMPION
and CHRIS MARTIN